RIVER FOREST PUBLIC LIBRARY

3 1865 00195 5680

W9-ARD-656

RIVER FOREST PUBLIC LIBRARY
735 Lathrop Avenue
River Forest, Illinois 60305
708 / 366-5205

5/09

Invertebrates

Sea Stars, Sea Urchins, and Their Relatives

Echinoderms

Beth Blaxland
for the Australian Museum

CHELSEA HOUSE
PUBLISHERS
An imprint of Infobase Publishing

RIVER FOREST PUBLIC LIBRARY
735 Lathrop Ave.
River Forest, IL 60305

This edition first published in 2003 in the United States of America by Chelsea House Publishers, a subsidiary of Infobase Publishing.

Reprinted 2003, 2004, 2005, 2007, 2009

All rights reserved. No part of this publication may be reproduced or transmitted in any form or by any means without the written permission of the publisher.

Chelsea House Publishers
An imprint of Infobase Publishing
132 West 31st Street
New York, NY 10001

You can find Chelsea House on the World Wide Web at http://www.chelseahouse.com

Library of Congress Cataloging-in-Publication Data Applied for.
ISBN 978-0-7910-6996-7

First published in 2002 by
MACMILLAN EDUCATION AUSTRALIA PTY LTD
15–19 Claremont St, South Yarra, Australia, 3141

Copyright © Australian Museum Trust 2002
Copyright in photographs © individual photographers as credited

Edited by Anna Fern
Text design by Polar Design Pty Ltd
Cover design by Polar Design Pty Ltd
Illustrations by Peter Mather, Watershed Art and Design
Australian Museum Publishing Unit: Jenny Saunders and Kate Lowe
Australian Museum Series Editor: Deborah White
Australian Museum Scientific Adviser: Dr Penny Berents

Printed in the United States of America

Acknowledgements
Cover photograph: Sea star, courtesy of Karen Gowlett-Holmes/Nature Focus.

Alex Steffe/Lochman Transparencies, p. 11; Clay Bryce/Lochman Transparencies, pp. 15, 16, 23, 24, 27, 29 (top); Eva Boogaard/Lochman Transparencies, pp. 9 (bottom), 17, 18, 19, 28; Jeremy Colman/Lochman, p. 7 (bottom); Peter & Margy Nicholas/ Lochman Transparencies, pp. 3, 9 (top), p. 14; Carl Bento/Nature Focus, p. 25; Karen Gowlett-Holmes/Nature Focus, pp. 4 (all), 5, 6 (all), 7 (top), 8, 12, 15, 20 (all), 21 (all), 22 (all), 26, 29 (bottom), 30; Michael Aw/Nature Focus p. 10.

While every care has been taken to trace and acknowledge copyright, the publisher tenders their apologies for any accidental infringement where copyright has proved untraceable.

Contents

Glossary words
When a word is printed in **bold**, you can look up its meaning in the Glossary on page 31.

What are echinoderms?

Echinoderms are a group of invertebrate animals. An invertebrate is an animal that does not have a backbone. There are many different kinds of invertebrates. Some other examples of invertebrates are worms, snails and insects. Can you think of any other invertebrates?

There are different kinds of echinoderms, but all of them live in the sea. Four of the main kinds of echinoderms are:

◎ sea stars
◎ brittle stars
◎ sea urchins
◎ sea cucumbers.

> **Fascinating fact**
> There are about 6,000 different types of echinoderms.

Ⓐ **These sea cucumbers are echinoderms.**

Ⓥ **A sea star is an echinoderm.**

General features of echinoderms

Some kinds of echinoderms look very different from others. For example, sea stars look very different from sea cucumbers. Scientists put these different-looking animals into the same group because they are all closely related. Scientists know these animals are closely related because their bodies all have the same general features.

Sea stars, brittle stars, sea urchins and sea cucumbers are all echinoderms because they are all invertebrates that:

◎ have a hard skeleton under their skin

◎ do not have a head

◎ have a body plan based on a five-pointed star shape with a mouth in the center

◎ have many special little tubes called **tube feet** that they can stretch out of their bodies to help them move about or gather food.

⚠ **All echinoderms have tube feet. This sea urchin's tube feet are black and white. Some of its tube feet are stretched out farther than others.**

How do you say it?

echinoderms: *e-**ky**-no-derms*
invertebrate: *in-**vert**-a-bret*

Fascinating fact

Sea stars are sometimes called starfish, but they are not fish. Fish are very different from echinoderms. A fish is different from an echinoderm because a fish:
• is not an invertebrate
• has a head
• does not have tube feet.

Echinoderm bodies

Echinoderms are the only animals that have tube feet. An adult echinoderm does not have a head, but it does have a mouth. In most echinoderms, the mouth is found underneath the body. An echinoderm's body spreads out around its mouth and can be shaped like a star, round ball, flattened disk or sausage.

The bodies of sea stars, brittle stars, sea urchins and sea cucumbers each look a little different.

Sea stars

Sea stars have a flattened body with many arms that form a star shape. Some sea stars have five arms while others have more. The part of the body that is in the center of all the arms is called the **disk**. The arms and disk are often covered in many hard bumps or spines. The mouth is underneath the body, in the middle of the disk.

disk

arm

⋀ **This is a sea star.**

Did you know ?

One kind of sea star has 40 arms!

Brittle stars

Brittle stars have a flat body with a small circle-shaped disk and very long, thin arms. Most brittle stars have five arms but some have more. The arms often have many short spines on them. The mouth is underneath the body, in the middle of the disk.

⋀ **This is a brittle star.**

This sea urchin has thick spines.

Sea urchins

Some sea urchins have a ball-shaped body, but others are more flattened and disk-shaped. They do not have arms. A sea urchin's body is covered with many spines. Its mouth is underneath the middle of its body.

Sea cucumbers

Most sea cucumbers have a body that is shaped like a sausage. Some kinds of sea cucumbers have short, wide bodies and some have long, thin bodies. They do not have arms or long spines, but they can have small bumps or short spines on their bodies. Most sea cucumbers lie on their side with their mouth at one end. The mouth is surrounded by **tentacles** that can be stretched out to feed. At other times, the tentacles are pulled inside its body.

> **These are two sea cucumbers.**

Fascinating fact

Sea stars and sea cucumbers were given their names because of where they live and because of their shapes. Sea stars live in the sea and have a star shape. Sea cucumbers also live in the sea, and many are shaped like a cucumber.

This one has pulled most of its tentacles inside its body.

This one has stretched its tentacles out to feed.

Special features of echinoderm bodies

Tube feet

Adult echinoderms have tiny water-filled tubes called tube feet that help them gather food and move about. These tube feet can be stretched out through tiny holes in the skeleton. Some echinoderms have tube feet with little suckers on the ends that can grip onto things.

The tube feet of sea stars and brittle stars are found in rows that run along the bottom of their arms. In sea urchins, the rows of tube feet are found in lines that run down the sides of their bodies. Sea cucumbers have tube feet around their mouths and also in rows along the sides of their bodies.

V This is the underside of a sea star.

> ### Fascinating fact
> Echinoderms can stretch their tube feet out a long way by filling them with water. To make their tube feet shorter, echinoderms squeeze the muscles in the walls of their tube feet. This pushes the water out and their tube feet get shorter again.

rows of tube feet

The mouth is under the body, in the center of the disk.

Body plan

The bodies of most adult echinoderms are arranged in a star pattern with the mouth in the center. Often the star has five arms or points, but sometimes it has more. Sometimes the star pattern is hard to see and you need to look at the echinoderm's mouth, skeleton or organs inside its body.

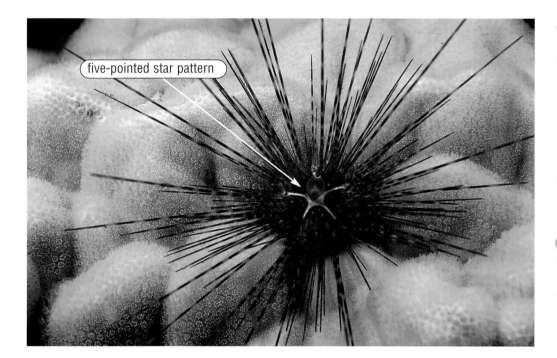

five-pointed star pattern

◁ **This is a sea urchin. If you look at the top of its body, you can see a star pattern. The star pattern divides the sea urchin's ball-shaped body into five parts. Each part is covered in long spines.**

▽ **This is the stiff skeleton of a type of sea urchin called a heart urchin. The skeleton shows a five-pointed star body plan.**

Skeleton

Echinoderms have a hard skeleton just under their skin. These skeletons are made up of lots of very small, hard plates. Sometimes the small plates join together so tightly that the skeleton and body are stiff and cannot bend. Sea urchins have a stiff skeleton with tightly joined plates. When they die, their skeletons keep their shape and are often washed up onto the seashore.

Other echinoderms do not have stiff skeletons. This allows their bodies to bend. This is very important for sea stars and brittle stars because they need to bend and twist their arms to catch their food and move about.

knobs where spines join onto the skeleton

holes for tube feet

The life cycles of echinoderms

Echinoderms have two kinds of life cycles. Most echinoderms have a life cycle that makes young echinoderms. These young echinoderms look very different from their parents. Some echinoderms have a different kind of life cycle. This life cycle does not produce any young. Instead, an adult echinoderm splits into two parts. Each new echinoderm then grows back its missing parts.

A life cycle with young

Most echinoderms make new echinoderms by sexual reproduction. Sea stars, brittle stars, sea urchins and sea cucumbers all **reproduce** in this way. This kind of reproduction needs two parents, but can make millions of new, young echinoderms.

V **Sometimes many males and females will come together to release their sperm and eggs into the sea. This makes it more likely that some tiny sperm and eggs will join to make new echinoderms.**

To reproduce, an adult female provides eggs and an adult male provides **sperm**. Many eggs and sperm are released into the sea at about the same time and place. This is called spawning and it usually happens once a year.

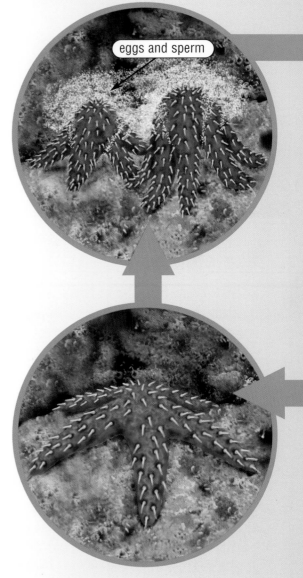

eggs and sperm

Young echinoderms reach their adult size when they are between two and five years old. The adult echinoderms are then ready to reproduce.

When an egg and a sperm join, a new echinoderm called a **larva** begins to grow. The larva looks very different from its parents and is so tiny that a **microscope** is needed to see it.

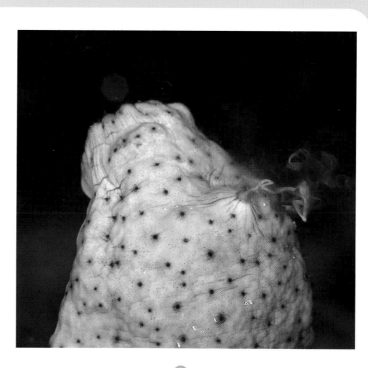

⚠ **This male sea cucumber is spawning.**

The larva swims about in the sea and grows bigger. After a few months, the larva's body changes to look like a tiny adult. At this stage, the young echinoderm starts to look like either a sea star, a brittle star, a sea urchin or a sea cucumber.

Fascinating fact

The word "metamorphosis" is used to describe the big change that happens when a larva changes into an adult.
Some other animals that go through metamorphosis are:
- tadpoles that turn into frogs
- caterpillars that turn into butterflies
- maggots that turn into flies.

How do you say it?

larva: *lar*-va
metamorphosis: *met-a-**morf**-o-sis*

A life cycle without young

Some echinoderms can also reproduce another way. These echinoderms can make new adult echinoderms without making young echinoderms. Only some sea stars and some brittle stars can reproduce this way. They break their bodies into two parts and then each new echinoderm grows back its missing parts. This kind of reproduction makes two echinoderms from only one parent. This means the sea star or brittle star does not have to find a partner before it can reproduce.

Did you know ❓

Some kinds of echinoderms live for less than ten years, but others live for about 35 years.

Ⓥ **One of these sea stars has just broken its body into two parts. Each part has only three arms. When all the missing parts grow back, the two new sea stars will each have six arms and a complete disk.**

First the sea star or brittle star breaks its body into two parts. These two parts can be about the same size, or one part can be much larger than the other. Each part must include some of the disk from the center of the body. If some of the disk is not present, then the sea star or brittle star cannot reproduce this way.

Each part then grows, or **regenerates**, the missing parts. It can take up to a year for these parts to grow back. These sea stars or brittle stars can look very strange while the missing parts are growing back.

When the two parts finish regenerating, there are two complete new adults instead of one. Sometimes the two new adults look exactly like the original parent, but sometimes the offspring grow back extra arms when they regenerate. Each adult is now ready to reproduce again. When they do reproduce again, these adult echinoderms can either regenerate or use sexual reproduction.

How do you say it?
regenerates: *ree-**jen**-er-ates*

Where echinoderms live

Echinoderms live in seas all around the world. Adult echinoderms live on the sea floor. They can be found on all kinds of sea floors, from the deepest parts of the sea to the seashore. Some echinoderms live in places where the sea floor is hard. Others live in places where the sea floor is soft.

Hard sea floors

Hard sea floors are made of rock or **coral**. Sea stars, brittle stars and sea urchins are often found living on rocky seashores, coral reefs and other places where the sea floor is hard. Many echinoderms find shelter in and under the rocks or corals.

Sea stars

Many sea stars and other echinoderms that live on hard rocks or coral reefs have suckers on the ends of their tube feet. These suckers help them grip onto the ground. Sea stars can crawl upside-down under rocks because their suckers can grip so well.

⋀ This sea star's tube feet enable it to crawl up rock walls and under overhanging rock ledges.

Fascinating fact

Echinoderm larvae float and swim near the surface of the sea, but the adults live on the sea floor.

Sea urchins

Sea urchins often seek shelter in small holes in rock or coral. Some even use their mouth to dig a small hole into the hard ground. They sit in the hole and hold on with their tube feet and spines so that waves do not wash them away.

> ▶ **These sea urchins live on a rocky seashore in small holes they have made in the rock.**

Brittle stars

Brittle stars often hide under rocks. During the day, they find dark places to hide. They come out at night to move about. Brittle stars lift their disk up off the ground and crawl on their arms. Small spines under their arms help them grip the rocks or corals as they crawl.

> ▶ **This brittle star's spines and tube feet stop it from slipping as it crawls over the rocks.**

small circle-shaped disk

long, thin arm

Soft sea floors

Some echinoderms prefer to live in places where the sea floor is soft. This soft ground is made of sand or mud. Some sea cucumbers, sea stars, brittle stars and sea urchins live in these places. Some live on top of the sand or mud and others burrow into the soft ground.

Sea cucumbers

Some sea cucumbers crawl on the sea floor, some sit on the sand and hardly ever move about and some burrow. When digging a burrow, sea cucumbers use their tentacles to help push the sand or mud away. Some sea cucumbers sit in their burrow with just their tentacles sticking out of the opening.

Fascinating fact

Many echinoderms have suckers on the ends of their tube feet. These suckers can only work if there is something hard to grip onto. Suckers cannot work on soft ground such as sand or mud because they cannot grip onto it.

Ⓥ **Sea cucumbers often sit on sandy sea floors.**

Sea stars

Many sea stars that live on soft ground do not have suckers on the ends of their tube feet. Instead, their tube feet have pointed tips. These tube feet help the sea stars dig down into the sea floor to find buried food.

Brittle stars

Most brittle stars like to hide in darkness. Some come out only at night. During the day, they hide under the sand or mud. It is always dark in the deep sea, and brittle stars that live in these deep places stay out all the time.

Sea urchins

Sea urchins that live on or in soft ground have a different shape from sea urchins that live on hard ground. Those that live on hard ground are shaped like a round ball. Those that burrow into soft ground have a flatter shape. Burrowing sea urchins also have shorter spines so that it is easier to burrow into the ground.

⚠ **This sea urchin burrows in sand. This kind of sea urchin is called a heart urchin. Its flattened body is covered in many short, brown spines.**

How echinoderms sense the world

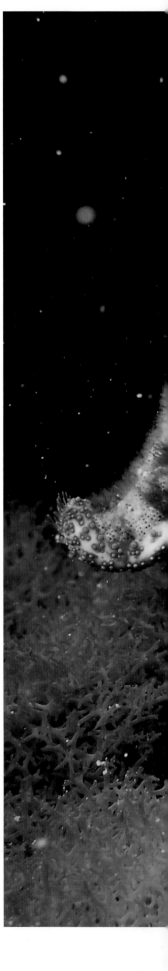

Echinoderms need to find out which way they should move to find food, and they need to know if there is danger nearby. Echinoderms do not have a head with eyes, ears, a nose and a tongue to help them sense things. They cannot see, hear, smell and taste things like humans can. Instead, they have different ways of sensing their surroundings.

Light

Echinoderms can sense light with their skin. Some echinoderms, such as sea stars and some sea cucumbers, also have simple eyes on their bodies. Echinoderms' eyes cannot see colors or shapes. They can only sense if their surroundings are light or dark.

Many echinoderms move away from the light. During the day, they like to hide in the shade in spaces under or between rocks. Other echinoderms move into the light.

Did you know ?

You can explore what it might be like to sense the difference between light and dark surroundings. Close your eyes and face a bright light. Keeping your eyes closed, cover your eyes with your hands. You should be able to sense when it is lighter and when it is darker. Echinoderms are much better than you at sensing light and dark. They can sense light with the skin all over their bodies.

Fascinating fact

A sea cucumber's eyes are found at the bottom of the tentacles around its mouth. The eyes of sea stars are under a small tentacle at the tip of each arm. Some sea stars turn the tips of their arms upwards so that their eyes face the light.

Smell

Echinoderms can smell or sense chemicals with their skin. Brittle stars and sea stars find their food by smelling it through the skin on their tube feet.

Touch

All echinoderms can feel things with their skin. This means they have the sense of touch. They can feel the ground they move over, the food they eat, and anything that touches them.

Gravity

Sea urchins and some sea cucumbers can also sense **gravity**. This sense lets them know which way is up and which is down. This is very useful for echinoderms that burrow under the sea floor. It lets them know if they are burrowing up or down.

◀ **This sea star is exploring its surroundings with its tube feet. The skin on its tube feet can smell and feel things. Its eyes are under a small tentacle on the tip of each arm.**

What echinoderms eat

Different kinds of echinoderms eat different foods. Some echinoderms eat plants, some eat animals and some eat tiny bits of food that they find on the sea floor or in the water.

Brittle stars

Adult brittle stars gather tiny bits of food from the water or from the sea floor. They use their tube feet to pick the food up and pass it along to their mouths. If they find larger bits of food, they use their arms to sweep the food into their mouths.

> This arm is curled around some larger bits of food.

⋀ **This brittle star is lying in the sand with three of its arms waving about in the water to collect food.**

⋀ **The bodies of these sea cucumbers are buried under the sand, but their tentacles are stretched out to gather tiny bits of food from the water.**

Sea cucumbers

Adult sea cucumbers use the tentacles around their mouths to help them eat. They stretch out their tentacles and pick up little bits of food from the water or the sea floor. Then they suck the food off their tentacles and into their mouths.

Fascinating fact

Echinoderm larvae eat tiny plants and bits of food floating in the water. A microscope is needed to see both the larvae and their food.

Sea urchins

Some adult sea urchins eat little bits of food in the water or on the sea floor. Others eat plants such as seaweeds or seagrasses. Sea urchins cannot bend their bodies, so they often have to crawl on top of their food before their mouths can reach the food. Then they use their hard teeth to scrape the food up into their mouths.

This sea urchin has rolled itself up in some seagrass and it also has a piece in its mouth. Its tube feet hold onto the seagrass as it eats.

Did you know ?

Some animals have a shell to protect them, but many sea stars can open these shells. The sea stars grip the shells with the suckers on their tube feet and pull the shells open. Then they push their stomachs out of their mouths and into the shells to eat the animals inside.

Sea stars

Many adult sea stars are **predators**. They eat small invertebrates such as snails, oysters, clams, crabs, worms and other echinoderms. They have to crawl on top of their **prey** before they can eat it.

Some sea stars swallow their prey whole and spit out any hard shells or other pieces they cannot eat. Others push their stomachs out of their mouths and over their prey. Then they digest their food by turning it into a liquid. This can take many hours. When they have finished feeding, they pull their stomachs back inside their bodies.

This is the underside of a sea star that has caught a sea snail to eat. The sea star has pushed its stomach out of its mouth and is starting to wrap its stomach around the sea snail.

stomach

How echinoderms defend themselves

Most echinoderms are quite small and slow. This means it is hard for them to scare away predators or to quickly escape from danger. Instead of being big or fast, echinoderms have other ways to defend themselves.

Spines

Many echinoderms have hard bodies covered in spines. Spines help to keep predators from getting too close. Some echinoderms have short spines and others have long spines. Some have spines that are thick and strong, while others have spines that are thin with very sharp tips. Some have spines with poison in them.

◁ **This sea urchin has two kinds of spines. The longer spines are thick and strong. The shorter, yellow spines are thin and needle-like. They can cause painful wounds if they are touched.**

Hiding

Many echinoderms hide from their predators. They hide in small cracks in the rocks or in burrows under the ground. Some echinoderms hide all day and only come out to feed at night when it is hard for predators to see them.

Many echinoderms have colors and patterns on their skin that make them hard to see against their surroundings. This **camouflage** is another way to hide from predators.

⋀ **Find the brittle star in this picture. It is sitting on some soft coral, but the colors and patterns on its body make it hard to see.**

Escaping

Some echinoderms are able to escape from their predators. These echinoderms can make a predator slow down or even stop chasing them. For example, some sea cucumbers shoot out sticky threads from their bodies. These threads wrap around the predator and slow it down. While the predator tries to untangle itself, the sea cucumber escapes.

 These white threads are very sticky. Sea cucumbers can shoot them out to tangle a predator.

Brittle stars can also escape from their predators. If a predator grabs a brittle star by one of its arms, the brittle star will break this arm off its body. The brittle star then escapes while the predator is busy eating the arm that the brittle star left behind. Later, the brittle star slowly regenerates its missing arm.

Did you know ?

The word brittle means something that is easily broken. Brittle stars were given their name because of the way that their arms break off when they are touched. They do this to defend themselves from predators.

Sand dollars are sea urchins. They are different from many other sea urchins because their bodies are not shaped like a round ball. Sand dollars have flattened disk-shaped bodies. Their bodies are covered with short, thin spines that look a bit like hair. Most sand dollars are less than 5 inches (12 centimeters) wide, but some kinds can grow bigger.

Sand dollars live in seas around the world. Most live in places where the sea floor is made of sand or mud. They use their small spines to help them move about and dig burrows into the soft ground.

When they burrow in the ground, sand dollars feed on tiny pieces of food mixed in with the sand and mud. They use their tube feet to push this food into their mouths.

V This sand dollar has a flat body covered in short brown spines. It lives in shallow water, where it burrows into sand.

dollars

mouth

▲ **The top of a sand dollar's skeleton (right) has a pattern on it that looks like a flower with five petals. The bottom of the skeleton (left) has a hole in the middle. This was the sand dollar's mouth.**

Dead sand dollars are sometimes washed up onto the seashore after storms. Often, the only parts that get washed up are the skeletons, because the spines fall off and the soft body parts rot away.

The skeletons of sand dollars are interesting to look at. The top of a sand dollar's skeleton has a pattern that looks like a big flower with five petals. If you look closely, the petal pattern is made by many tiny holes in the skeleton. When it is alive, the sand dollar stretches its tube feet through these tiny holes.

Did you know ❓

Sand dollars were given their name because their flat skeletons sometimes look like large, round coins. Some people have other names for sand dollars. Some large, flat and yellow sand dollars are called sea pancakes. Some dark-brown sand dollars are called sea biscuits. Some sand dollars have large keyhole-shaped holes in their skeletons. These sand dollars are sometimes called keyhole urchins.

The crown-of-thorns sea star is one of the world's largest sea stars. It has many arms and is covered in long, sharp spines. Most adults grow to about 12 inches (30 centimeters) wide, but some grow as large as 32 inches (80 centimeters) wide.

Crown-of-thorns sea stars live on coral reefs in the Pacific Ocean and Indian Ocean. The larvae feed on tiny plants floating in the sea. By the time they are six months old, the larvae have changed into young sea stars that eat corals. When crown-of-thorns sea stars eat corals, they suck out the corals' soft bodies and leave their hard, white skeletons behind.

Fascinating fact

Crown-of-thorns sea stars can move 65 feet (20 meters) in one hour. This is fast for an echinoderm.

Did you know ❓

When it eats, a crown-of-thorns sea star pushes its stomach out of its body and over a piece of coral. It takes about five hours to eat its meal of coral. Then it pulls its stomach in and moves on.

🔺 **This crown-of-thorns sea star is eating corals. The white parts show where the crown-of-thorns sea star has eaten the coral animals, leaving their white skeletons behind.**

thorns sea star

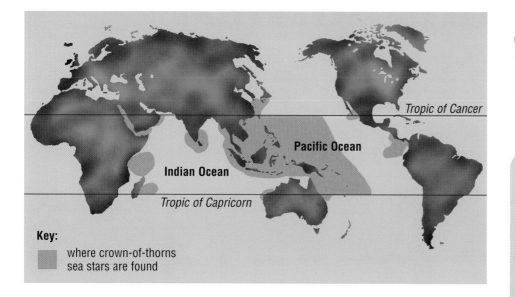

Key:
▪ where crown-of-thorns sea stars are found

Tropic of Cancer

Pacific Ocean

Indian Ocean

Tropic of Capricorn

◀ **Crown-of-thorns sea stars live in warm places throughout the world.**

Fascinating fact

One female crown-of-thorns sea star can produce about 60 million eggs during a spawning season. Only some of these eggs grow into adults. The rest are eaten by predators or die in other ways.

Crown-of-thorns sea stars are poisonous, and this stops many animals from eating them. There are some animals that can eat crown-of-thorns sea stars, including some fishes, one kind of shrimp and a very large sea snail, the giant triton. The giant triton holds the sea star with its strong foot, then stretches its long feeding tube past the poisonous spines and into the sea star's body to eat the soft parts inside.

Thousands of crown-of-thorns sea stars can be found on a coral reef. Scientists call this an "outbreak." When there is an outbreak of crown-of-thorns sea stars, many corals are eaten and the coral reef changes. First, tiny green seaweeds grow on the white coral skeletons. Then other plants and animals start growing on top of the dead corals. After a year, new corals cover the dead corals. It can then take up to 15 years for these new corals to grow so that the reef has the same amount of living coral as it had before the outbreak.

▽ **This crown-of-thorns sea star is eating the last piece of coral still growing here.**

Where can you see echinoderms?

You can sometimes see echinoderms along the seashore. Rocky shores and coral reefs are best explored at **low tide**. The best time to discover anything that has been washed up on sandy beaches is just after **high tide**.

Sandy beaches and mudflats

Most echinoderms that live on sandy beaches or on mud flats burrow under the ground. But if you are lucky, you might see a sea star or sea cucumber as the tide goes out. Look along the beach where the waves have washed up seaweed and other matter. You might find a sea urchin or a sand dollar's skeleton.

Rocky shores and coral reefs

It can be hard to see brittle stars because they like dark places under rocks and in deep water. Sea cucumbers are often seen in the **tropics**, where they lie in shallow water. Sea stars and sea urchins are easiest to find.

Look closely – the sea stars and urchins may be sheltering in rock pools, under seaweed, in cracks in the rocks or under coral. They may even be camouflaged. If you find a sea star that does not have sharp spines, gently turn it upside-down and watch how it turns itself back up the right way. Look to see how it bends its arms and uses its tube feet to turn over.

⚠ **Sea stars can sometimes be seen on the seashore at low tide.**

Many echinoderms live on coral reefs.

Safety tips

- Make sure an adult is nearby when you explore seashores. Rocky shores can be slippery, and big waves sometimes crash over the rocks. An adult can watch out for big waves and help you explore safely.

- Some echinoderms should not be touched because they have sharp spines or little pincers with poison in them.

mouth

pincer

This sea urchin has pincers that look like little flowers on stalks. The sea urchin uses them to defend itself. They can inject a poison that is strong enough to kill a person.

Quiz

1 Is an echinoderm an invertebrate? Why?

2 Where is a brittle star's mouth?

3 Where would you look to find a sea star's tube feet?

4 Do echinoderm larvae look like their parents?

5 Where do echinoderms live?

6 Can a sea star's simple eyes see things like our eyes can?

7 Many sea stars are predators. What kinds of things do these sea stars eat?

8 What happens when a brittle star loses an arm?

9 What kind of pattern is on the top of a sand dollar's skeleton?

10 What do crown-of-thorns sea stars eat?

Challenge
QUESTIONS

1 How does an echinoderm make its tube feet longer?

2 What word do scientists use to describe the changes that happen when a larva turns into an adult?

3 If a sea star's arm was cut off its body, could the arm regenerate back into a whole sea star?

4 Do all echinoderms have suckers on the ends of their tube feet?

5 What happens to a coral reef when there is an outbreak of crown-of-thorns sea stars?

Turn to page 32 to check your answers.

> **This sea star is very colorful, but it is camouflaged in these surroundings.**

Glossary

camouflage	Colors and patterns on an animal's body that make the animal hard to see against its background.
corals	Tiny invertebrate animals that live in large groups and make coral reefs. There are soft corals and hard corals. Hard corals have rock-like skeletons that are often used as a habitat by other living things.
disk	The middle part of a sea star's or brittle star's body. The arms attach to the disk and the mouth is underneath the body, in the middle of the disk.
gravity	The power of Earth to pull things downwards. For example, if you jump up off the ground, gravity pulls you back down.
high tide	When the sea comes in and covers more of the seashore than at low tide.
larva	A young echinoderm. The larva looks very different from the adult.
low tide	When the sea goes out and leaves more of the seashore uncovered than at high tide.
microscope	A type of magnifying lens used by scientists to see very tiny things.
predators	Animals that hunt other animals to eat.
prey	Animals that are eaten by other animals.
regenerates	Grows back the missing parts of the body.
reproduce	To make more of the same kind of animal or plant.
sperm	Cells from a male animal's body that can fertilize the eggs from a female animal's body to reproduce.
tentacles	Parts of an invertebrate's body that stick out like fingers to sense things or gather food. Tentacles can bend and can often be made longer or shorter.
tropics	The part of Earth between the Tropic of Cancer and the Tropic of Capricorn, where air and water temperatures are always warm or hot.
tube feet	Tiny water-filled tubes that only echinoderms have. The tube feet can be stretched out through tiny holes in the skeleton and help the echinoderm gather food and move about.

Index

A
arms 6, 8, 9, 13, 15, 18, 19, 20, 23, 26

B
body plan 5, 9
burrow 16, 17, 19, 24

C
camouflage 22, 28, 30
crown-of-thorns sea star 26–7

D
disk 6, 8, 12, 13

E
eyes 18, 19

F
food 5, 8, 9, 16, 18, 19, 20–21, 24

I
invertebrate 4, 5, 21

L
larvae 11, 15, 20, 26

M
metamorphosis 11

P
predators 21, 22, 23
prey 21

R
regenerate 13, 23

S
sand dollars 24–5, 28
skeleton 5, 8, 9, 25, 26, 27, 28
spines 6, 7, 9, 15, 17, 22, 24, 26, 27, 29
suckers 8, 14, 16, 21

T
tentacles 7, 16, 18, 19, 20
tube feet 5, 6, 8, 9, 14, 15, 16, 19, 20, 21, 24, 25, 28

Answers to quiz
1 Yes, because an echinoderm is an animal that does not have a backbone.
2 Underneath its body, in the middle of the disk.
3 Underneath its arms.
4 No, the larvae look very different.
5 All echinoderms live in the sea and most live on or in the sea floor.
6 No. (They cannot see the shapes or colors of things. They can only tell the difference between light and dark.)
7 They eat other small invertebrates such as snails, oysters, clams, crabs, worms, corals and other echinoderms.
8 It regenerates, or grows back, the missing arm.
9 A flower pattern with five petals.
10 Corals.

Answers to challenge questions
1 It stretches them by filling them with water.
2 Metamorphosis.
3 No. (An arm cannot regenerate by itself. An arm needs to be joined to part of the disk to regenerate.)
4 No. (Many echinoderms that live on soft ground do not have suckers on their tube feet. Suckers only work when an echinoderm crawls over hard ground.)
5 These sea stars eat corals. When there is an outbreak, many corals are eaten and the coral reef changes. Other plants and animals start to grow, but it takes a very long time (15 years) for the reef to recover.